One Giant Leap

THE STORY OF NEIL ARMSTRONG

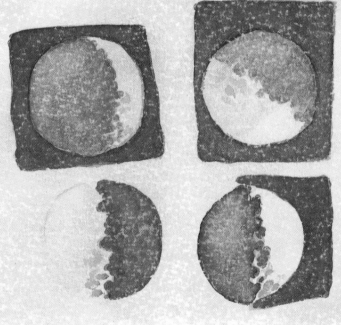

Phases of the Moon

AFTER GALILEO

Don Brown

Houghton Mifflin Company   Boston 1998

The text of this book is set in Frutiger.
The illustrations are pen and ink and watercolor on paper.

Library of Congress Cataloging-in-Publication Data

Brown, Don.
   One giant leap: the story of Neil Armstrong / written and illustrated by
Don Brown.
      p. cm.
   Summary: Discusses the life and accomplishments of astronaut Neil
Armstrong, from his childhood in Ohio to his famous moon landing.
   ISBN 0-395-88401-2
   1. Armstrong, Neil, 1930–   —Juvenile literature. 2. Astronauts—
United States—Biography—Juvenile literature.   [1. Armstrong, Neil,
1930–   2. Astronauts.] I. Title.
TL789.85.A1B76   1998
629.45'0092—dc21
[B]   97-42152
                                                                         CIP
                                                                          AC

Manufactured in the United States of America
BVG 10 9 8 7 6 5 4 3 2 1

To Sheahan and Corey.
They are the moon and the stars to me.

In 1932, two-year-old Neil Armstrong watched airplanes race.

Small, brightly colored planes flashed over Neil and his father, Stephen. The planes raced around a triangle-shaped course, their propellers tearing the sky with a sound that was like an endless thunderclap.

The spectacle surely left its mark on young Neil. Four years later, he leaped at the chance to ride in an airplane.

It wasn't on a racing plane but a three-motored passenger plane nicknamed the Tin Goose. The plane offered rides at the town airport. It could carry about a dozen people.

Neil and his father climbed aboard and buckled themselves into wicker seats. The engines sputtered to life with a terrific noise. The airplane raced down the runway and slowly lifted into the sky.

As the ground dropped farther and farther below them, people, houses, cars, *everything* looked smaller. The Tin Goose plowed through the clouds as gusts of wind bounced it up and down.

The noisy, bumpy ride and ever-tilting view worried Stephen Armstrong.

But Neil was fearless.

Neil was delighted.

Neil started making ten-cent airplane models and reading flying magazines.

He also started having a magical dream. In it, he held his breath and hovered above the ground. Below him, people, houses, cars, *everything* looked smaller.

As Neil grew, so did his interest in flying. Hundreds of model airplanes and stacks of *Air Travel* magazine began to appear in his bedroom.

A job mowing the Mission Cemetery lawn helped pay for it all.

At about the age of eleven, Neil worked for Neumeister's Bakery. Because he was small, Neil was placed into the dough-mixing vats to clean them.

He dreamed again and again of hovering.

When Neil was thirteen, the Armstrongs moved into a big white house on Benton Street in Wapakoneta, Ohio. Neil had been born in the living room of his grandparents' nearby farm on August 5, 1930.

Neil was shy and made friends carefully. Still, his life was busy. There was school and Boy Scouts. He played baritone horn in the school band and in a group called the Mississippi Moonshiners.

He flew rubber-band powered airplanes from a grassy hill.

He worked at the West End Market and Bowsher's Hardware, and he swept up and stocked shelves at Rhine and Brading's Pharmacy on Main Street.

On clear nights, Neil climbed to the roof of his neighbor Jacob Zint's garage. Mr. Zint had a homemade telescope mounted there and welcomed visitors to spy the moon and stars.

Nell looked and looked and looked.

A few miles from the Armstrongs' home, down the old brewery road, was the Port Koneta airport. Neil went there to watch the planes take off and land. Sometimes people paid him to wash their planes.

But watching and washing was not enough. Neil asked his parents if he could learn to fly. The lessons cost nine dollars an hour. He would have to work twenty-five hours to earn enough for one hour of flying.

His parents agreed.

Soon afterward, Neil squeezed himself into a tiny Aeronca Champion airplane with his teacher, Aubrey Knudegard.

He learned to take off and land.

He learned to climb and swoop and bank.

He learned to follow a figure-eight path in the sky.

He learned that a pilot and an airplane together could be more than the person or the machine was alone.

Neil Armstrong earned his student pilot's license on his sixteenth birthday. He was too young to have an automobile driver's license.

In time, Neil Armstrong, student pilot, became Neil Armstrong, navy fighter pilot in the Korean War. Then he was Neil Armstrong, test pilot, flying rocket-powered airplanes to the upper edges of the sky. Eventually he became Neil Armstrong, astronaut.

Astronauts are special pilots who fly spacecraft around Earth. When Neil became an astronaut there was a plan to land people on the moon and then return them safely to Earth. The moon had gripped people's imagination for thousands of years.

On July 16, 1969, astronauts Neil Armstrong, Buzz Aldrin, and Mike Collins sat in a cramped capsule atop a Saturn rocket. The Saturn was as big as an office building and powerful enough to fling three people more than 200,000 miles to the moon!

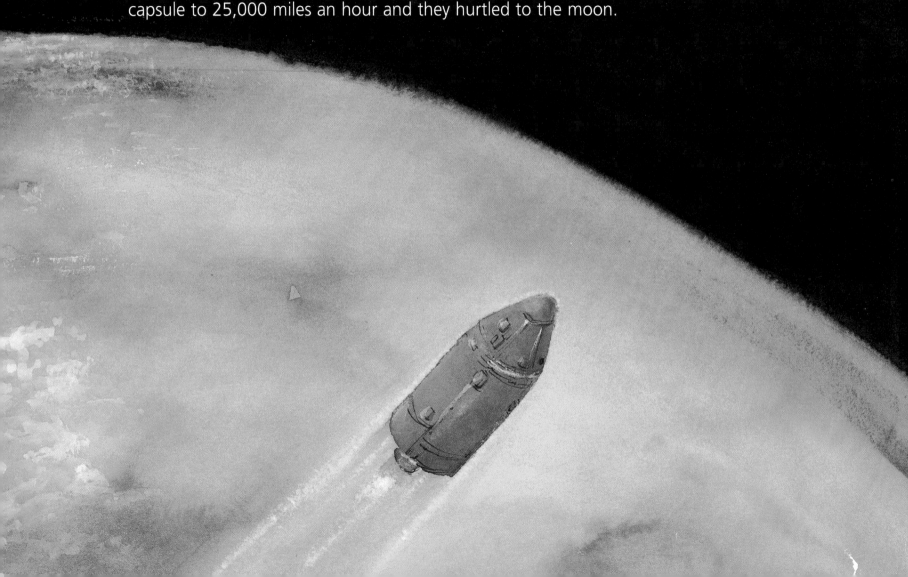

At 9:32 A.M. the main rocket motors erupted. Flames spewed from the Saturn's tail as it lifted from the ground. Soon the first set of engines exhausted their fuel and fell toward the ocean. Smaller engines sprang to life and sent the capsule circling the globe. After two turns around Earth, a final rocket engine blasted the capsule to 25,000 miles an hour and they hurtled to the moon.

Neil, Buzz, and Mike sped through black space for four days. The sun's light was broiling hot. The shadows were brutally cold. To prevent one side of the capsule from becoming overheated or frozen, it was turned slowly, like a hot dog on a grill. The astronauts called it the "barbecue roll."

When they reached the moon, Neil and Buzz entered a special spacecraft designed to part from the main capsule and land on the moon. Mike remained aboard the main capsule to pilot it as the other two astronauts dropped to the moon's surface.

A computer guided Neil and Buzz. But as they neared landing, Neil saw that there were large boulders in their way. He took control of the craft and slipped it over the obstacles. While he searched for a safer place to land, an alarm blared, warning that they were low on fuel. With only seconds of fuel remaining, Neil safely lowered the hovering spacecraft to the moon's surface.

Earthlings Neil Armstrong and Buzz Aldrin had finally reached the moon!

Wearing space suits and helmets, they opened the hatch of the spacecraft. Before them was the moon, magnificent and empty. Neil climbed down a ladder and hopped to the ground. Special cameras allowed 600 million people on Earth to watch and listen.

"That's one small step for man, one giant leap for mankind," Neil said into his microphone.

He gathered moon rocks for scientists to study later. As he worked, his boots left marks in the dust. Neil's footprints may remain there for a million years. There is no wind, no rain, and no snow on the moon to disturb them.

Buzz climbed down the ladder and stepped onto the moon's surface.

Earth hung above them in a perfectly black sky. North Africa could be seen behind swirling white clouds.

Neil shuffled over the powdery surface toward Buzz. The sun shone with a bright white light.

Neil stood next to Buzz. Their helmets almost touched. Buzz grinned broadly. Neil clasped his hand on his partner's shoulder.

"Isn't it *fun!*" Neil said.

On July 20, 1969, Neil Armstrong stepped on the moon and became a hero to millions of people.

But inside him was the memory of an ordinary boy from Wapakoneta, Ohio.

A boy who loved books and music.

A boy who was shy and who made friends carefully.

A boy who dreamed of hanging in the air suspended only by a trapped breath.